Kingussie

At the Head of the Pines

Kirks, Castles
and Characters

John Robertson

Uiga Robertson

Uiga and John Robertson

Contents

Copyright © Uiga & John Robertson, 2002

First Published in 2002
by Kingussie Millennium Committee

ISBN 0952 4642 36

Complete origination and printing by Farquhar & Son Ltd, Perth

Kingussie

LEAN GU DLÙTH RI

CLIÙ DO SHINNSRE

Follow closely the fame of your fathers

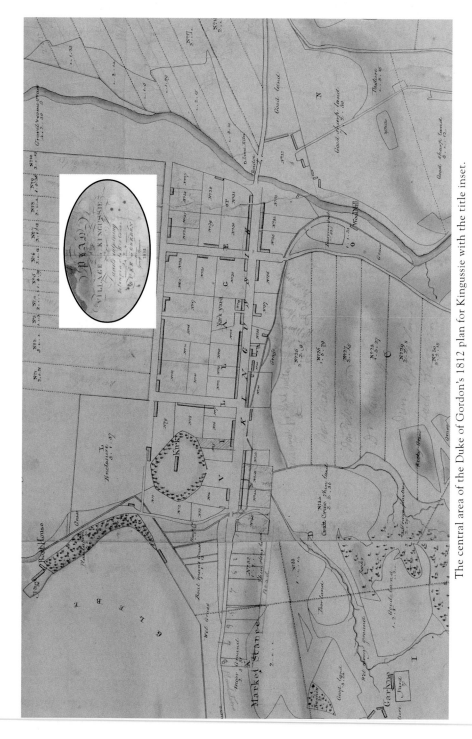

The central area of the Duke of Gordon's 1812 plan for Kingussie with the title inset.

Acknowledgements

This publication could not have taken place without the financial assistance of Awards for All Lottery Fund, Community Economic Development Fund and Highland Council (Badenoch & Strathspey area).

The authors would like to thank many people for kindly providing photographs. Firstly, Sallie Chase for the gift of a collection of photographs which belonged to her mother, Lilian Martin. We are grateful to Kingussie Tennis Club, Donnie Anderson, Alasdair Cameron, Gillean Clark, Alasdair Duff, Alistair McCook and Rod Maclean for access to their collections. Our thanks to Kingussie High School and to Kingussie Primary School for providing many groups, some of them taken by the late G D Wilson, which should bring back many memories.

In its 125th year Kingussie Bowling Club kindly allowed us to use some of its photographs. Special thanks to Martin Robertson for assistance and access to his collection of photographs.

In addition the following people have generously helped: Bette Armstrong, Sandy Bennett, Duncan Cameron of "Flying Cameras", Rachel Chisholm of Highland Folk Museum, Jim Dallas, Irene Dallas, Mary Dean, Isabel Denoon, Margaret-Ann Gilbert, Nicky Gow, Donnie Grant, Trudy Healas, Cath Hunter, John Lawson, Gordon Lennox, Miriam Longstaff, Morag MacKintosh, Bert Mark, Sandy McCook, Barbara Maclean, Donald MacLeod, Allan Macpherson-Fletcher, Chrissie Macpherson, Pete Moore, Shirley Nield, Frances Porter, Ailith Stewart, Joe Taylor and Tom Wade. Also, Martin Grant of H. Tempest Ltd and BBC Scotland.

For the 1812 Plan of the Village of Kingussie our thanks to Bill Campbell and Bob Steward and to Ewan Weatherspoon for photographing it.

Every effort has been made to ensure the correct spelling of names throughout the book. In the event of mistakes the authors offer their apologies.

Valentine images are reproduced by kind permission of St Andrews University Library from postcards published by James Valentine & Sons, Dundee.

The proceeds from the sale of this book go to the Kingussie Millennium Fund.

Foreword

This second collection of photographs from the Kingussie Millennium Committee offers images of the town and surrounding area from 1860 to the present day.

I would like to congratulate the authors on this fascinating collection of 300 photographs, most of which are previously unpublished, and I highly recommend it as a permanent reminder of the buildings and characters in our Highland town.

Provost Tom Wade, 1969

The recent discovery of a plan of Kingussie dated 1812, and the gift of a large collection of photographs from Sallie Chase, gave the authors the incentive to produce this book. By publishing these pictures the Millennium Committee has created a valuable record of the culture and heritage of Badenoch that can be enjoyed by generations to come.

Residents of Kingussie, past and present, exiles and regular visitors owe a debt of gratitude to Uiga and John Robertson, and to the Millennium Committee for this truly remarkable collection of photographs.

This book provides a visible link between the present and the past, and so it is with great pleasure, a sense of belonging and a touch of nostalgia, that I recommend and endorse this collection.

I hope you enjoy it as much as I have.

Tom Wade

Introduction

Clearing out my late mother's house in Edinburgh, I came across cases of books and photographs relating to the Highlands. My mother, Lilian Martin, came to live in Kingussie from the south of England during the late 1940s and remained there for nearly 20 years.

She was a keen gardener, making a lovely garden at our home, the Old Chapel House, (the present library) opening it for visitors to walk around. Any donations put in the "wee tin" at the gate went to the Shinty Club funds. She was a founder member of the Horticultural Society, doing many broadcasts for the BBC.

Her great interest in history helped her to become one of the founder members of the Badenoch Field Club. The Field Club, once formed, had speakers and lecturers during the winter months, while in summer they did field trips in Dean's Buses, visiting sites of historical interest.

With the late Mary Lumsden, (Dean), my dearest friend, I took a trip down 'memory lane' in 2001 when we met with John Robertson and passed on to him many photographs and recollections of our magical childhood. We spoke of the pantomime my mother wrote and produced in the Victoria Hall; performing in 'Little Women' at the Drama Festival; learning Highland Dancing with Nan Gibson; dancing with the Pipe Band; shinty matches followed by dancing in the Drill Hall; modelling clothes with my sister, Vicky, at the Highland Folk Museum for their postcards and many other topics.

Kingussie is a wonderful place to grow up and live in. I hope my mother's collection of photographs helps to bring back happy memories.

Sallie Munro (Chase)

In 1999 a plan of Kingussie, dated 1812, was discovered in Dellifour House. The plan, drawn up for the Duke of Gordon, is of interest because it shows his intended layout of the new village. A point to note is that it has been drawn with south at the top.

Mr Campbell, who found the plan, gifted it to the Highland Folk Museum in Kingussie where it is available for examination. His discovery provides an appropriate starting point for this book.

2002 is a special year in Kingussie's history with the construction of the new Badenoch Leisure Centre on the site of the Victoria Hall, destroyed by fire on 1st August 1999. It is an astonishing coincidence that the Victoria Hall was built in 1887 to celebrate the Golden Jubilee of Queen Victoria and 115 years later a new hall is being built on the same site in the year of Queen Elizabeth's Golden Jubilee.

Most of all, this book is about recording the images that give a Highland town its identity and if this has been achieved in any small way then it will have been a success. We hope that for many years to come these pictures will be a reminder of the **kirks, castles and characters** that give Kingussie its unique heritage.

It has been a privilege to compile this collection of images and the authors are grateful to the many people who have assisted.

In the Shadow of Creag Bheag. Kingussie, 2002.

In The Beginning

Gynack Bridge and the approach to Kingussie from the south.

High Street c. 1870 This early photograph was taken before the British Linen Bank, the present Bank of Scotland, was built in 1876.

Early Kingussie before the railway and the terraces were built. c1860
The original Free Church was at right angles to the current Free Church.

Kingussie. c1900

Building the Highland Railway line at the north end of Kingussie in 1863. The inscription on the original photograph reads "The Coffee Pot" - perhaps referring to the tender.

A well-earned rest whilst constructing the railway.

A parade in the High Street before the Star Hotel was opened. c1870

The Star Hotel has replaced J A MacKintosh's shop in this picture. The post card trade was obviously popular in Crerar's corner shop. Many old postcards of Kingussie bear either his name or that of J Johnstone.

A full stand at the Badenoch and Rothiemurchus Highland Games at the Dell. c1910
The stand collapsed in 1932.

Kingussie Secondary School soon after opening in 1876. The railings were used for scrap metal in the Second World War and were only replaced in 1995. Many public buildings such as the Victoria Hall lost ornamental railings which have never been replaced.

A Territorial Army camp in 1917 at the Speyside Distillery, now Ardvonie Park.
They were probably on a route march as part of their summer training.

Soldiers leaving Kingussie Station for service in the 1914-18 war.

Three men, deep in conversation, approach the Duke of Gordon Hotel. c1910

A pony and trap at the top of Gynack Street. c1900.

Hope it doesn't rain! The Caberfeidh Stage Coach prepares to leave Kingussie bound for Fort William.

Looking along Spey Street from the Gynack Bridge.

Soldiers in King Street. c 1940

Parade during the visit of King Edward VII, High Street, 1909.

The calm before the storm. The evening before the arrival of Edward VII at the Duke of Gordon Hotel.

King Edward VII's car approaches the Duke of Gordon Hotel, 1909.

A procession in the lower part of the High Street. c1900

The High Street in 1910

The Kingussie Pipe Band leads a procession in the High Street. c1925

A leafy scene
on Spey Street
looking towards
the Highland Folk
Museum.

Kingussie from
Creag Bheag
during tree
felling.

The view of the town looking east from Creag Bheag.

Kingussie Parish Church from East Terrace before a porch was added to the entrance.

The Catholic Church of Our Lady and St Columba, 1932.

The first grave-stone at the churchyard was erected in 1815 for infant, Katherine Booker, who died whilst on holiday. It was twelve years before the second burial took place at St. Columba's Church.

The Star Hotel's yard before the garage was built.

Pram at Kingussie Station. Trainspotting?

The Independent Order of Good Templars
at Kingussie in 1890s.

Posing for a photograph in front of the Smiddy

West Terrace, Kingussie and Creag Bheag.

The message on this Christmas card reads: "Hope to be home soon".

Kingussie Primary School pupils at the Dell, 1918,
celebrating the end of the Great War.

Edwardian Style: Misses Hogarth, Warren, Russell, MacDonald, Fraser and Troup, 1909.
Miss Fraser collected photographs of Kingussie. Some from her collection feature in this book.

John Clark with assistant Duffy McKinloch
outside the Jeweller's in 1901.

Alex Freckie at his draper's shop
in the High Street, c1900.

High Street, 1930s.

A Good Scottish Education

Marking the Centenary of the Education (Scotland) Act which made education compulsory for all.
Provost T. R. Wade, M. Grant (Headmaster), N Wade, Rev N. Wright, J. McArdle.

Former pupils, staff and pupils at the Centenary of the opening of Kingussie Secondary School, 1976.

Mhairi Hughes and John Taylor add the finishing touches to a mural depicting life in 1876, while Helen Edwards and Caroline Waller are seen printing commemorative carrier bags.

Primary pupils in Victorian costume
at the Centenary Sports Day.

Jackie Bennett in Victorian dress on Centenary Day, 1976.

Dinner ladies Margaret Macpherson, Mary Fraser, Nan Maclean and Mary MacQueen prepare lunch in the new High School kitchen.

Learning the basics - Jill Cameron, Alison Mackenzie, Frances Munro and Alison Dallas

Rev D K MacLeod, Free Church Minister, with Primary 7 Quest Club. 1981

Stylish dancing girls
(left to right)
K. Maclean, J. Mackie,
J. Norton, P. Watson, C.
Wade, A. Porter, B.
Maclean
Front: J. Dobbie

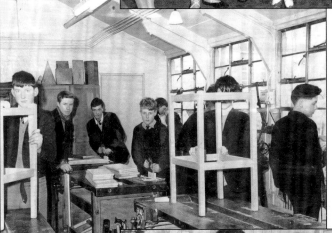

Woodwork Class.
A stark contrast
to today's hi-tech
facilities.

Nature Study!

Primary prize-winners, 1973

Mrs A Gunn with Primary 2 showing off their project 'Kingussie at the Turn of the Century', 1976.

Chef, Jock Russell, looks on while Headmaster, William Anderson, addresses the Haggis.

Visiting speaker, Norman McCaig, Scottish poet (4th from right), at a Burns Supper in 1975.

A Singing class
in the old school.

Gymnastics at
Kingussie School
1960s.

Taking to the air!
Long Jump at Kingussie
School, 1965.

Primary 2, 3
and 4 girls in
1957

Presentation
time at
Kingussie
High School

Celebrating
the end of
term!

Beyond the Boundary

An early picture of the Square in Grantown-on-Spey.
The tall building was built as an orphanage in 1824 by Lady Jane Grant.

Duncan Macpherson with his mother outside their shop at Drumguish.

Invereshie House.

Sir George Macpherson-Grant's coming of age party at Invereshie House.

The winding road through the village of Aviemore c1906. Strange to think this was part of the Great North Road.

Aviemore House, later known as the Home Farm, was demolished in the 1960s.

Demolition in progress.

Newtonmore Main Street.

St Columba's Church was situated
at the top of Station Road,
Newtonmore.

The United Free
Church,
Newtonmore.

Newtonmore Village Hall, built in 1913.

Insh Village c1900.

Balavil House.

Victorian party outside Balavil House c1880

Balavil House the day after a damaging fire in 1903.

Sweeping the chimneys at Balavil – not for the faint-hearted!

The sluice gates at Loch Morlich. The sluice gates were used to raise the level of the loch to create a head of water to float timber from Glenmore down the rivers Luinneag and Spey to Spey Bay for ship building.

The ferry which was replaced by the bridge at Boat of Garten.

Sallie Chase, Mary Dean, Sheena Innes and Margaret Urquhart dancing at Kinrara House in 1953.

An accident near Ruthven caused great interest when the road collapsed.

Dalwhinnie c1925

Holiday Inns

A Stage Coach leaving the Duke of Gordon Hotel, 1895.

The Royal Hotel c1930.

The Star Hotel and the High Street.

The Mains Hotel, Newtonmore.

Rowanlea Hotel, Newtonmore, now the Glen Hotel.

Anderson's Hotel, Newtonmore.

The Balavil Hotel, Newtonmore, before the front porch was extended upwards.

Lynwilg Hotel,
once a famous
coaching Inn

Aviemore Station Hotel.

Pot Luck Tearooms, Aviemore.

The Palace Hotel and Gardens,
Grantown-on-Spey.

The Old Bridge
and Hotel,
Carr Bridge.

Nethy Bridge Hotel.

Times to Remember

Scottish Community Drama Association. The Gynack Junior Team in "Little Women" adapted from Louisa M. Allcott's book by Lilian Martin, 1953.
Back L-R: Sallie Chase, Vicky Chase, Dawn Robertson, Middle: Mary Dean, Margaret Urquhart, Christine Innes, Front: Kathleen Maclean.

Sunday School Picnic.

A bird's eye view of Kingussie during a Gala Day at the High School in 1995.

Enjoying the sunshine on Sports Day at Kingussie High School, 1980.

Kingussie Gala Day, 1950s.

Obstacle Race on Sports Day.

Canadian Mounties visit Kingussie Primary School. Looking on are: I. Kaye (Burgh Surveyor), M. Grant (Headmaster), Bailie Mrs Whyte, Provost T. Wade, R. Maclean (District Clerk).

Philip Cameron and Ali John
Campbell in tandem in 1995.

Shirley Nield, the organiser, at the start of the 2001
Bikeathon in aid of Leukaemia Research.

Ready to go! Bikeathon 2001 which raised £32,000. The total for 2002 was £36,000.

Pipe Band leading the British Legion to the War Memorial in Gynack Gardens, 2000.

Drumhead Service at the War Memorial in 2000 led by Rev Helen Cook.

The opening of the new Cairngorm Mountain Rescue base at Rothiemurchus, April 2001.

John Allen, leader of the Cairngorm Mountain Rescue Team, with well - known climber Hamish MacInnes, April 2001.

Blind Date! Arthritis Care Fun Night at the Lodge Hotel, Newtonmore, March 1996.

Penny Collection. Alvie Primary School raised £34 in June 1995.

Centenary Celebrations at St Vincents in June 2001. The grandson of the founder, Dr Walter de Watteville, and his wife cut a cake to mark the occasion.

Enjoying a Strawberry Tea in the sunshine.

Victorian Lady, Ann Hay.

Graceful dancers entertain the crowds.

Storm clouds gather over a Gala Day at Kingussie High School in 1995.

The new
extension to
the Surgery
nearing
completion,
March 2001.

Doctors Michie,
Anderson and Munro
with Mrs Dunbar at
the opening of the
extended Kingussie
Medical Practice.

Runners passing Viewfield Filling Station, 1995.

Cyclists approach Feshiebridge on
a tour of Speyside, June 1995.

A Burns Supper in Kincraig in 1996. David Mackintosh
addresses the haggis, watched by Susan Kennedy and
piper, Sandy MacDonell.

The Duke of Gordon Hotel rebuilt after the fire of 1996, with the old play equipment at Ardvonie Park in the foreground.

Installing new play equipment in March 2001.

Watched by a jester, Anne Lorne Gillies entertains children at an Open Day in the Highland Folk Museum, 1985.

The end of an era in 1996. Macrae's joinery workshop before being dismantled and reassembled in the Folk Park. L-R: Stephen Whymant, Councillor Sandy Russell, Ross Noble, Helen Powell and James MacDonald (former manager of Macrae Builders).

Badenoch Gardening Club and Newtonmore Floral Art Club Annual Show in the Village Hall, Newtonmore, 1995.

The chairlift on Cairngorm soon after opening in December 1961.

Bob Clyde explains a technical point to the Duke of Edinburgh watched by Archie Scott, at the lower station, Cairngorm, 1970.

Councillor Bob Severn and Avril Gibson look at plans for the proposed Funicular Railway, 1998.

The arrival of the carriages of the Funicular Railway at the bottom of the track on Cairngorm, October 2001. It opened for business 40 years after the chairlift.

A day out of school!

A Fashion Show in Kingussie High School.

Another smash hit, *Oliver* – December 1977. L-R: Stephen Booth, Penny Raetty, John Renton (Oliver), Kevin MacDonald and Alan McKie.

A presentation of Gilbert and Sullivan's *Mikado* in the Victoria Hall in the 1920s.

Sandy Russell poses for Coia in Newtonmore
watched by Jack Richmond and friends, 1983 . . .

. . . the Finished Article.

Road-widening on Tait's Brae in 1983.

Construction of the new A9, 1970's.

Pupils show off their Christmas cards at Kingussie's Christmas Shopping Day, December 2001.

Harry Potter and Santa Claus – one of the popular attractions at the successful Sunday Shopping Day in December 2001. This has become an annual event in Kingussie's calendar.

Ruthven Barracks, 2000.

One of the first renderings of *Flower of Scotland* was at Ruthven Barracks in 1960's.

The opening of the new police station in 1973 by Provost T. Wade – Front Row (l-r): Superintendent J. Cunningham, Mr F.F. Bruce, Ex-Provost Mrs M. Murphie (Ft. William), Provost T.R. Wade, Mr D. MacDonald, T. MacKenzie, Bailie Mrs M. Whyte, Mr A.L. McClure, Major A.C. Robertson M.B.E.

Highland Games

It's a fair cop! Tug of War in Ardvonie Park depicting the winning team. c1970.

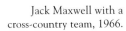

Jack Maxwell with a cross-country team, 1966.

Willie Murchie presenting the School Sports Trophy to James Carr.

Step Dancing class led by Maggie Moore at Feis Spe, 1996

Fly-tying class at the
Wade Centre in 1996.

Collision Course! Sandy
Bennett takes the particulars.

Strathspey Thistle Rugby Club 2002 - L to R standing: Les Hargreaves, Graeme Cuthbert, Iain
Cornfoot, Paul Cobb, Martin MacKenzie, Gary Taylor, Sean O' Brian, Kenny Knox, Davie Orr,
Lloyd Humphreys, Pete Moore, Neil MacDonald, Dave Kinnear, Kenny Deans, Dave Reive, L to R
kneeling: Simon Newman-Carter, Matt McGrath, Steve Ethridge, Dougie Langlands (Capt), Mark
Lynch, George Byers, Jimmy Whyte, Grant Davis. Highland District League Winners 2002.

A Ploughing Match at Balavil.

Badenoch & Strathspey Welfare League Champions 2002.
Kingussie C. Meeks, Roseannagh Mackie, P. Mathewson, G. Macrae, I. Borthwick, S. MacWilliam, D. Borthwick, C. Dawson, C. Mitchell, R. Grant, G. Brown, P.Gow, R Selvester, S. Morrison.

Bob Beck presents the Football Shield to Gary Dallas, 1982.

Welfare league football at the Market Stance.

Anyone for Tennis? Tennis Champs of 1940s.

Tennis Tournament, 1982.

Shinty 1964: Back- A. Dawson, W. Thomson, A. Taylor, D. Wright, E. Fraser, S. Falconer, N. MacWilliam. Front – A. MacIntyre, T. Nolan, D. MacDonald, A. Wolfe, L. MacIntyre.

Pay attention boys! Jack Maxwell with orienteering group.

Preparing for a Musical, 1980s

Badminton – Back: D. MacDonald, M. Binnie, A. Muir. Front: M. Longstaff, J. Robertson, J. Renton.

Jock Russell instructs Ian Binnie and David Walters in the ancient art of fencing, 1974.

A bit of a racquet! Back: M. Allen, M. Falconer, K. Thain, R. Cameron, N. Robertson, G. Gray, D. Cumming. Front: E. Abercromby, S. Campbell, L. Dallas, J. MacDonald, F. Kinnear, J Gordon, ?, J. Gibson. 1980

Happy faces! Winners of the Mackay Cup held by A. Anderson, front left, and several other trophies in 1975.

Skiers Keep off the Greens! 1999.

Norman MacWilliam.
In 2002, he had won 12 Club
Championships and 9
Kingussie Opens.

Fashion in Golf attire in 1915.

Golf Club House, Kingussie c1920.

Bill Longstaff, takes to the air above Glen Feshie.

Girls Hockey Team, 1964.

Kingussie under 14, Ken MacMaster Cup winners with Oban at An Aird, Fort William, 1994.

Kingussie Sports Winners, 1977 – Back: I. Mackintosh, A. Prochazka, P. Hartman, A. Macrae. Front: R. Fraser, E. Morrison, C. Sefton, S. Cook.

STRATHSPEY and **BADENOCH** HER

INCORPORATING THE STRATHSPEY HERALD AND THE BADE

THURSDAY, AUGUST 4, 1988

h Deposit
r Clubs

USSIE football
shinty club
s deserve a real
n the back for
recent fund-
efforts, which
et to swell each
coffers by
d £700.
nd £1400 was
from an
al competition in
the public were
to "Pick A Pet"
bstantial £500

idea was to pick
bered square on
ssie   Stance
ll ground on

An inconvenient wait for George Nicholson, left, and Douglas Campbell, who had money on Daisy the cow doing the business in Kingussie Shinty Club's novel fund-raiser on Sunday.

A moo-ving target!
Fund-raising in 1988.

Aerial view of Dunbarry shinty pitch, used when the Dell was being resurfaced, 1992.

The Six-in-a-row team. Camanachd Cup Winners 2002. Back: G. Munro, T. Nolan, S. Borthwick, C. Dawson, J. Hutchison, P. Gow, I. Borthwick, P. Davidson, I. Anderson, A. Borthwick, R. Dallas, J. Gow, A. MacLeod, M. Davidson, M. Sinclair. Front: K. Thain, D. Borthwick, E. MacKintosh, A. Dallas, R. Ross, M.Clark, R. Fraser

Speyside Distillery's R. Christie presents S. Borthwick, A.Dallas and D. Borthwick with commemorative Quaichs to celebrate their achievement of winning a record number of Camanachd winner's medals (13). 2002

Primary Shinty Team at the clubhouse with Alan Dawson.

Donnie Grant with Denise Lewis, Olympic Gold medallist, at the Dell, 2001.

Macpherson Cup Winners

Back: M. Fraser, G. MacDonald,
I. Macpherson, R. Muir,
I. Campbell, A. Young.
Front: G. Macpherson, F. Nield,
E. Tait, A. Macpherson,
G. Begg, M. Mackay.

The height of fashion on the
Bowling Green in the 1930s.

Encouragement at a Bowling Match, 1936

Photo time in 1956: L. McEdward.
seated: M. Maclean, Mrs Hood,
W. Brewis. Front: Nancy Hood.

The Bowling Club celebrated its 125th Anniversary in 2002.
This picture, taken in 1890 in front of the original clubhouse, indicates the popularity of the game
from the start.

Mrs Hutchison throws the first bowl of the season

Georgina Maclean, a stalwart of the Bowling Club.

An inter-club match in the 1950's L to R: W. Carrick, visitor, visitor, W Maclean, visitor, J. Gunn, G. MacBean, visitor. In background: T. MacArthur, J. Denoon.

Familiar Faces

Dr Orchard makes a presentation to Willie Maclean on his retiral from the Bowling Club.

A young Dr Orchard admires his father's new car.

Dr I.F. Grant out for a spin!

Dr I. F. Grant, who founded the Highland Folk Museum in Kingussie in 1944, outside one of the Black Houses.

Kingussie Church of Scotland Women's Guild Sale of Work in 1974. Back row (from left): Mrs M. Falconer, Mrs A.D. Hutchison, Mrs J. Cumming, Mrs H. McCann, Mrs M.E. Thomson, unknown, Mrs L. Vaughan and Mrs I. Jenner. Middle: Mrs C. Macpherson, Mrs R. Smillie, Mrs M. Taylor, Mrs P. Mackay, unknown, Mrs I. Flint, Mrs D. MacDonald, Front: Miss D. Milne, Mrs B. Maclean, Mrs L. Macpherson, Mrs T. Kerr, Mrs V. Maclean, Mrs J. Todd, Mrs C. Hunter, Mrs A. Macleod, Miss J.F. Cameron, Miss L. Farquharson and Mrs L. Fraser.

Kingussie Secondary School Staff, June 1969. Back: N. Gunn (Secretary), J. Russell, J. Strathdee, D. Banks, M. Fraser, M. Mackenzie, D. Wilson, D. Bruce. Middle: J. Cuthill, French Assistante, A. Abercromby, M. Donald, A. Stanners, M. Porteous, J. Maxwell, A. Gunn, R. Kirk, J. MacGillivray. Front: J. Todd, G. Maclean, R. McCann, C. Macpherson, M. Grant (Headmaster), J. McArdle (Depute), C. Cameron, J. Moir, J. Todd.

Mrs Orchard presents a Certificate to
Ranger Guide, Rachel Simpson,
September 1969.

Brownies studying Avionics, September 1969.

Badenoch Pipe Band, 1994.

An annual outing of the Kingussie St Andrews Church Choir in the early 1930s. Standing, from left: Ian Millar, T.R. Paton (town clerk), E. Barron, I.B. Johnstone, W.R.F. MacGillivray, W. Ritchie (bus owner), Miss Dutch, F.W. Millar, Rod Maclean, Mr Dutch, Miss Dutch. Seated: Bunty Millar, Mrs Paton, Evan Cattanach, Mrs Millar, M. Barron.

Standfast 1921. Silverfjord Hotel in background.

U. F. Church - Band of hope, Back: A. Falconer, ?, B. Falconer, M. Cowie, R. Maclean. Front: J, MacDonald, J. Gibson, A. Cameron, W. Maclean, H. Fraser.

Kingussie High School Drama Club.

That windswept look! 1976 Division 3 Champions and Sutherland Cup Winners. Back: D. Thomson, J. Gow, A. Falconer, T. Gallagher, S. Dey, A. Ness, D. Grant, S. Borthwick, Front: W. Dallas, J. Clark, R. Falconer, G. Macpherson, C. Sharp, J. Cruickshank.

J. Gow, MacAulay Cup Winner 1983.

Saturday 15/11/97 - Shinty/ Hurling International at Oban Scotland v Ireland. Stephen Borthwick from Kingussie who was declared Man of the Match.

Camanachd Cup winners, 1984.

Donald MacKintosh, the AA Scout, sets off on patrol to Drumochter.

Traveller, "Tom the Grinder", sharpening knives, 1970.

"Wee MacGregor", sitting in front of Kingussie snowplough.

The Class of '53. **Back**: D. MacLennan, J. MacLean, H. MacDonell, ?, A. Maclean, R. Fraser, D. Taylor, ?, K. Davis, T. Porter, G. MacDonald. **Front**: B Nield, ?, T. Wade, ?, J. Dobbie, E. Mackay, S. Gordon, G. Christie, M. Davis, A. Maclean, S. Jeffries.

A presentation to the Town Clerk in 1975 before the reorganisation of Local Government. L-R: T.M. Robertson, U. Robertson, Major Robertson, A. Murdoch, T.R. Wade (Provost), N. Wade, A. Russell.

Office Bearers of the Church of Scotland - R. Maclean, W. Johnstone, J. Moir, S. Meade, J. MacGillivray. Seated: Rev. A. Jenner, Provost T. R. Wade, 1975.

Presentation to Mrs Dorothy Dean by Provost T. Wade in the 1970s.
Looking on are: R. Maclean, Councillor A. Russell, A. Murdoch, I. Dean, B. Millar, Dr I. Richardson, M. Orchard.

The full complement, 1974. **Back row L-R**: Paul MacKintosh, Jock MacKintosh, William Stewart, Tommy McCorquodale, Kenny Newbigging, Jim Thomson, Robbie Smart, Alistair Henderson, Fred Thomson, Sandy Bennett. **Middle row:** Norman McLeod, ?, Bob Severn, Fraser Beaton, Ian Smart, Angus McLean, Alec McLean, Alex Henderson, Alec MacDonald. **Front row:** Helen Morrison, Sandy Ross, George Paton, John Maclean, Simon MacDonald, Grace Panton, Christine Stewart.

St. Vincent's Centenary Celebrations, 2001.
Les Hargreaves and Calum Macrae

Friday 31/10/97 Kingussie Festive
Lights Auction in the Silverfjord Hotel
with Philip Cameron, left, Irving
Selvester, front and Kenny Reid.

A little more my way! Problems erecting a marquee for a
Rugby Tournament, August 2001.

Kingussie Shinty
Captain, Ali Dallas,
releases 1000 table
tennis balls on Tait's
Brae as part of a fund
raiser. September
2001.

Fire practice at Kingussie High School: R. Macpherson, A. Fell, G. Macrae. August 2001.

Calum Macrae and Sandy Bennett on the daily watering round, summer 2001.

Watched by his colleagues, Jackie Gibson receives a golden axe from Firemaster B. Murray at a presentation in the Star Hotel to mark his retirement from the Fire Service after 27 years of distinguished service.

A Touch of Frost

Looking South from
Creag Bheag after a heavy fall of
snow in January 2002.

Course Closed!

Gynack Road, December 1977.

High Street in winter, 1910.

The Caravan Site
at the Golf Course.
1950's

Gynack
Bridge, 1960.

Morning sunshine on Gynack Road, c1920.

West Terrace, Kingussie, looking across the Spey, c1910.

Flooding at Lynchat, 1989.

Muddy Waters!   The Gynack in flood, July 2002

The Gynack in spate at the Mill, 1920.

Summer shearing at Balavil.

The Great North Road winds its way to Newtonmore.

Creating the duck pond at the Glebe, August 1994.

Summer colour in the Centenary Gardens with the former Episcopal Church and the Victoria Hall in the background, 1992 .

Morning light on Ruthven.

The Old School Brigade

2001 **2002**

This unusual photograph involved the whole school of 400 pupils.

Kingussie High School Staff, 1994

Back row, L-R: Stuart MacIntyre, Adrienne Devlin, Colin Scott, Ken Deans, Dick Webster, Trevor Morris, Jim Campbell, Bert Mark, Gordon Stewart, Kenny Reid. Third row: Jack Maxwell, Dot Moyce, Irene Dallas, John Crombie, Lois Ballantyne, Phyllis Henderson, Julia Macadie, Audrey Cumming, Brian Dziennik, Marilyn Scott. Second row: Alison Shaw, Willie Anderson, Sheena Duthie, David Taylor, Kenny MacIntyre, Duncan Wink, Jim Ballantyne, Shirley Nield, Lesley Dyce, Mairi MacKay. Front row: Jane Wallace, Jenny Dunn, Hilary Fisher, Troudel Kuntz, Andrew Dunn (Depute), Dr Tom Taylor (Rector), Theo Whiteside, Ailith Stewart, Muriel Hunter, Uiga Robertson, Elspeth MacDonald.

Kingussie Primary School Staff. 2002

Back: A. Urquhart, J. Maclean, P. Derbyshire, P. Brown, A. Munro. Middle: K. Anderson, M. Geddes, P. Garrow, R. Orr, M. Dawson, S. Riley, A. Thom. Front: R. Bootle, R. Cameron, M. Maxwell, P. Lockhart (Head Teacher), J. Steinle, T. Cuthbert.

The Class of '86. Back: D. Robertson, O. Russell, J. Falconer, K. Baxter, M. Bambury, S. Ross. Middle: M. Selvester, M. Murray, M. Shaw, A. Shaw, C. Mort, D. Dunn, K. Robertson, S. Shaw, J. MacBeth, H. Campbell. Front: R. Conner, D. MacDonald, S. Leslie, F. Cromarty, G. Macrae, M. Davidson, J. Gibson, E. Bulmer, C. Meeks.

Flocking to school?

The Music Festival Prize-winners, Kingussie, 1969.

The Music Festival, Primary 2, 1978. Back row, L-R: Stuart Gilmour, Anna Cumming, Julie Eley, John McPherson, Philip Cairney. Middle: Samantha Mort, Michael Bennett, Jennifer Kinnear, Lorraine Muir, Karen Meeks, Lisa Falconer, Nicola Clark, Stacey Ross, Murdo Shaw, Douglas Cameron. Front: Siobhan Ogilvy,Samantha Matheson, Alex Wilkie, Gary Duffus, Graeme Condie, Paul Clark, Peter Leslie, Robert Moir, Steven Gilmour.

Music Festival Prize-winners, Kingussie 2002. Back row, L-R: Scott Pirie, Duncan Fraser, Gemma Menzies, Rona Skuodas, Ruth Blackshaw, Craig Myerscough. Front row: Calum Wardrope, Gary McIsaac, Kirsty Graham, Lindsay Simpson, Connie Johnson, Sarah Grant, Andrew Rossi.

Primary 1 at play in 1973.

Gymnastics for Primary 2 in 1977. On wall bars: Karl Falconer and Linda Thain. L-R: Cathy Ross, Rupert Reeves, Virginia Levack, Becky Wood, Maureen Shaw, Karen Young.

Separate Tables! Making paper chains for Christmas decorations. Back row, L-R: Anne Cattanach, Heather Harrold, Moira MacWilliam, Robert Cooper (at sink). 2nd Back row: Peter MacDonald, Morag Davies, John Harling. 3rd Back row: Anne Grant, Callum Stewart, Finlay MacIntosh, Donald Kennedy. Front row: Julian Renouf, Alec Campbell.

Primary 1 with Miss Filshie, 1981. Back row, L-R: Paul Nield, Barrie Dallas, Ian McMillan, Alistair Munro, James Maclean, Duncan Leavitt, Mark Eley, Josie Clyde. Front row: Fiona Moore, Lucy Don, Nicky Cromarty, Vicky Boyle, Laura Kearns, Nicky McRae, Stephanie Nolan, Louise Clark.

Friday playtime for Primary 1, 1980. L-R: Paul Gilchrist, Julie McMillan, Elizabeth Bennett, Paul Mathewson, Rosalind Hamilton.

All collars and bows. Miss MacLennan's class of 1902/03.

Staff of Kingussie Public School, 1909.

Staff in 1920.

A Right Royal Occasion

Her Majesty, The Queen, accompanied by Provost George Miller in Grantown-on-Spey, 1961.

Queen Elizabeth, The Queen Mother, admires a glass decanter at the Aviemore Trade Fair watched by, left, Colin Ferres, Caithness Glass and right, David Pirnie, Managing Director, Craftpoint, Beauly.

Prince Philip with Lord MacDonald at Newtonmore Village Hall, 1961.

Kathleen Gower (nee Maclean) and her husband Christopher being introduced to The Queen in the 1970s. They were guests at a reception in Halifax, Nova Scotia, on the Royal Yacht, Britannia, which then sailed to New York.

Her Majesty, The Queen, with Gordon Bentley at Highland China, Kingussie, 1983.

Queen Elizabeth, The Queen Mother, at a trade fair in Aviemore. 1980's

Coronation Garden on Kingussie High Street in 1952. The colour scheme was red, white and blue.

The Queen is amused by the animals at Highland China.

Rod Maclean wearing his Silver Jubilee medal with King Olav of Norway.

Alistair McCook, MBE, outside Buckingham Palace, 2002.

A colourful display in Gynack Gardens for the Queen's Golden Jubilee, 2002

Setting off on a Duke of Edinburgh Award Scheme exercise.

Let's have a rest!

A fine place to pitch our tents.

Eat your heart out, Jamie Oliver!

Following in the Footsteps

A Highland Township, c1700, recreated at the Highland Folk Park, Newtonmore.

Water-powered saw bench
at the Folk Park.

Transport is laid on for those unable to walk round the Folk Park. In the background is an example of a prefabricated church. Along with schools and village halls these were common sights in rural areas of the Highlands.

The main panel of the Millennium Tapestry, created by Kingussie Stitchers, currently hanging in the Area Office of Highland Council.

Quality Awards presentation in 1999 to the Highland Folk Museum. L-R: A. Simpson, Councillor A. Gordon, H. Powell, B. Powell, G. Watson, S. McRobert, R. Noble, R. Chisholm

Around the Shops in 2002

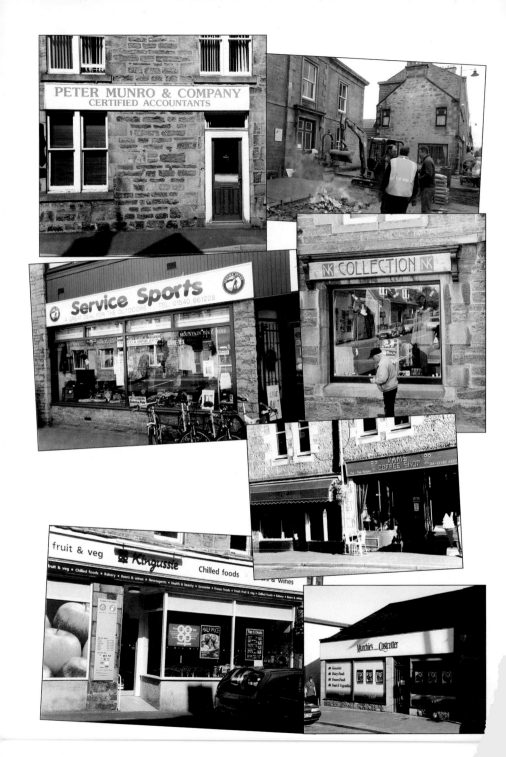